Benjamin Moseley

A treatise concerning the properties and effects of coffee

Benjamin Moseley

A treatise concerning the properties and effects of coffee

ISBN/EAN: 9783741136672

Manufactured in Europe, USA, Canada, Australia, Japa

Cover: Foto ©Andreas Hilbeck / pixelio.de

Manufactured and distributed by brebook publishing software
(www.brebook.com)

Benjamin Moseley

A treatise concerning the properties and effects of coffee

A TREATISE

CONCERNING THE

PROPERTIES and EFFECTS

OF

COFFEE.

———

THE FIFTH EDITION,
WITH CONSIDERABLE ADDITIONS.

———

By BENJAMIN MOSELEY M.D.

Physician to Chelsea Hospital, Member of the College
of Physicians of London, of the University of Leyden,
of the American Philosophical Society, &c. &c.;
Author of a Treatise on Tropical Diseases, Military
Operations, and the Climate of the West-Indies.

———

LONDON:

PRINTED FOR J. SEWELL, NO. 32, CORNHILL.

M.DCC.XCII.

PREFACE.

THE reception which four editions of this Treatife have met with, has made it neceffary to publifh a fifth; which I now prefent to the reader, with fuch additions, as I hope will be accceptable and ufeful *:

I HAVE collected many authorities, to corroborate what I have advanced; that, as my opinions have prejudices to contend with, they may not, however, be objectionable on the ground

---

* The firft Edition was publifhed in the beginning of 1785.

of

of fingularity, and . be confidered as
fupported by no other teftimony than
my own.

In treating of the falutary advantages, which the public will derive,
individually, from the general ufe of
Coffee, it is impoffible not to reflect
alfo on the political benefits which
will accrue to the Parent State, by increafing its cultivation in her Colonies.

To the Colonifts themfelves the
object is very extenfive; and furely
the profperity of fo important a part
of the empire, as our Weft Indian
Iflands, demands the moft liberal attention on the part of the nation.

From

FROM the produce of our Plantations, that " magnificent property," as Monf. NECKER terms the French Colonies, " which only the fuperficial and ignorant affect to undervalue," this country receives great additions to her revenue, and a total fupply of one of the moft ufeful articles (perhaps now a neceffary) of life. Yet, from the calamities lately inflicted on fome of them by the hand of Providence, and the accumulated burthens which the public neceffities have laid on them all, many of the Planters are involved in ruin; and thofe who efcape muft owe their deliverance to the braveft ftruggles of induftrious virtue.

THE

THE population of White Inhabitants, which is the great fecurity of the Iflands, confifts chiefly of thofe who cultivate the inferior Staple Commodities, among which, Coffee is now the principal; and this population has always been proportionable to the increafe or decreafe of thofe Staples. Indigo may be inftanced as an example: When Indigo was encouraged in Jamaica, before that impolitic duty was laid on it, which exterminated the cultivation of it in our Colonies, and gave it to the French, there were confiderably more White Inhabitants in that Ifland than there are at prefent, though the Ifland. now prcduces five times the

quantity

quantity of Sugar and Rum it did at that time.

THE cultivation of Coffee requiring but little capital, is an inducement for people of fmall fortunes to fettle in the Iflands. It is a creditable refuge for the induftrious man, who has been unfortunate in Trade, and to thofe whofe larger fchemes in life have failed. — It is an eafy employment; the labour light, and many parts of it performed by children. The fituations and foil where it is carried on muft be dry, and of courfe healthy, to be advantageous. Coffee Plantations, in particular, may be confidered as a Nurfery of ufeful Inhabitants for the Colonies.

The

The foil beft fuited for Coffee is happily fuch as can be fpared from every other purpofe. Large tracts of poor land, which would otherwife lie wafte and ufelefs, may be rendered as profitable as the beft, without the mortality and cafualties attendant on fevere labour in hot climates.

The numerous little families which live on Coffee Plantations, and are difperfed in fmall fettlements, in the interior parts of the Iflands, occafion the mountainous and woody lands to be cleared and opened; and to be interfected with roads and eafy communications.

THUS

Thus the residents live in safety, and all sorts of property acquire a proportionate value and security. The retreats of fugitive negroes are laid open; plunder and depredation prevented; and conspiracies for rebellion are deprived of their hiding-places.— And thus the credit of the planter, and security of the merchant, stand on a firm basis:—those commotions being prevented, which have so often disturbed the tranquillity of the Islands, and occasioned the ruin of many individuals abroad and at home, to the great defalcation of that immense revenue, which these Islands pay to the Mother-Country *.

Besides,

---

* The duties and excises, upon a computa-

tion

BESIDES, the importance of a numerous body of men, to form an occasional militia, is evident, to any person acquainted with the Colonies, who muſt know how little fatigue and expoſure to the ſun is ſufficient to deſtroy an unſeaſoned ſtranger.

INHABITANTS are always ready in caſe of ſudden emergency; and being acquainted with local circumſtances, and inured to the climate, can perform ſervices, which uninformed, raw, European troops cannot do; and, were intereſt and attachment leſs operative con-,

tion for the year 1781, amount to about £. 1,344,312 ſterling, annually, on the produce of *Jamaica* only.

ſiderations,

fiderations, Colonial Inhabitants may be depended on; — many inftances of which were exhibited in the events of laft war.

THE firmnefs difplayed by the militia of Jamaica, during the different periods of Martial Law at that time, when left almoft to defend themfelves, ought ever to be remembered to their honour. While many of the troops that were raifed here with fo much difficulty, and fent thither and maintained at fo much coft, were perifhing in hofpitals, the Ifland militia underwent the fevereft fatigues, with the greateft alacrity; chiefly at their own, and, let me add, very heavy expence, I was then Surgeon-General of the Ifland, and had the care of the militia,

litia, and likewife the camps of the regulars, and witneffed the facts I relate.

THE truth is, that Sugar Plantations, though they are great fources of wealth to their proprietors, as well as to government, do not employ a fufficient number of white people for their internal fecurity, againft the infurrections of the negroes. The manufacture is fimple, and the labour wholly carried on by flaves; and though the Deficiency Law of Jamaica directs, that one white perfon fhall be employed for every thirty flaves, under a penalty of thirty pounds per annum for every deficiency,—yet, this law is often defeated, or the fine fubmitted

fubmitted to; as white fervants are expenfive, and a lefs number than that proportion is fufficient for the purpofe of making Sugar.

THE cultivation of inferior Staple Commodities is therefore neceffary to the very exiftence of the Sugar Colonies; and I am perfuaded will prove to them more beneficial in many refpects, than at prefent is generally imagined.—Here, then, is an open and grateful field for Colonial Patriotifm; in which the *Amor Patriæ* will neither find oppofition from envy, nor difappointment from ingratitude.—Here is the occafion to demonftrate the love of country, and to perpetuate a benefit to mankind, which will never be forgotten;

gotten; and if thofe who, from cha-
racter and fituation are entitled to attention, will come forward, and point
out to the Public the impofitions it has
fuffered from mifreprefentations, and
that the interefts of the Sugar Colonies
are no other than the beft interefts of
this Country, there will never be
wanting fufficient good fenfe in the
Nation, to underftand, that a fubject
of the realm, exerting his induftry at
four thoufand miles diftance, may be
employed as beneficially to the State,
as the manufacturer at home, who
lives by him; and is as much deferving
the protection of it, as the Country
'Squire, who leaves his fox-hounds, to
give a filent vote or two during the
winter, and retires the remainder of
the

the year to his *Sabine Fields* in sloth and ignorance.

Sir Nicholas Laws was the first person who planted Coffee in Jamaica; —but dying three years afterwards, in 1731, he had not the happiness to see the cultivation of it make any considerable progress.

In 1732, several of the Planters and Merchants, belonging to the Island, became patrons of the undertaking; and convinced that, under proper encouragement, it might be of importance to the Island, and that Coffee might become a flourishing staple article of produce, they subscribed the

sum

fum of 220 l. 10 s. towards defraying the charges of foliciting an act of parliament for lowering the inland duty, upon the importation of Coffee from Jamaica into Great Britain; which at that time was 10 l. fterling per cwt.

The circumftance being but little known at prefent, and confidering what obligation the Ifland is under to their exertions, I am happy in having an opportunity of inferting their names, as a proper tribute to the memory of thofe benefactors to the Colony, and friends to the Nation.

LONDON,

LONDON, *Anno* 1732.

A Lift of the perfons who fubfcribed and paid into the hands of Mr. *Roger Drake and Co.* the feveral fums undermentioned, towards defraying the charges of an application, for an Act of Parliament, to encourage the planting of *Coffee* in the Ifland of *Jamaica*.

	£.	s.
John Afcough, Efq;	10	10
Thomas Beckford, Efq;	10	10
James Dawkins, Efq;	10	10
Henry Dawkins, Efq;	10	10
Meff. Drake, Pennant, and Long;	21	0
Thomas Fifh, Efq;	10	10
Mr. James Fitter;	5	5
Cope Freeman, Efq;	10	10
John Gibbon, Efq;	10	10
Mr. John Gregory;	5	5
Capt. Jofeph Hifcox;	10	10
Mr. Henry Lang, and Co.	5	5
James Lawes, Efq;	10	10
John Lewis, Efq;	10	10
Mrs. Sufannah Lowe;	10	10
Samuel Long, Efq;	10	10
Charles Long, Efq;	10	10
Meff. Mayleigh and Gale;	10	10
Valent. Mumbee, Efq;	10	10
Favcle Peeke, Efq;.	10	10
	10	10
Capt. George Wane;	5	5 .

£. 220   10

IN

In the fame year, and in confequence of this folicitation, the *Act* 5*th* *Geo.* II. was paffed, entitled, " An Act for encouraging the growth of Coffee in the Plantations in *America*." —The preamble recites, that the foil and climate of Jamaica are particularly adapted for the growth of this commodity; and the act itfelf reduces the inland duty upon Britifh Plantation Coffee, imported into Great Britain, from two fhillings to eighteen pence per pound: — And here it ftood for many years, producing a revenue of about 10,000l. per annum. A few years ago, on the reprefentation of the Weft Indian Planters, *Lord John Cavendifh*, the then

Chan-

Chancellor of the Exchequer, consented to the very important reduction of one shilling more; thereby furnishing a most useful lesson to all future financiers, — *the present duty of six pence per pound actually producing nearly three times the sum that was received when the duty was eighteen pence:* so true is the doctrine, that heavy taxation defeats its own purpose.

It has been computed, that one acre of land will contain 1100 Coffee plants, which will produce berries in eighteen months from the sowing of the seed. The trees will continue bearing for seven or eight years.— Each tree, after the first bearing, may

b   produce,

produce, at a medium, one and an half or two pounds weight, one with another; and fix or eight fervants can manage ten or twelve acres, befides cultivating provifions for themfelves. Upon this ground of calculation, it is apparent, that one acre of land, fuppofing the weather not unfavourable, may yield annually from 1700 lb. to 2200 lb. weight, which, when brought to market, may fell for 9l. 15s. to 12l. 15s. fterling *net*. This, it is true, is but a fmall profit; for it is little more than five farthings per pound, whereas the *duty alone is fix pence per pound*. If the duty was equalized to that upon Sugar, the medium profits per acre would be about 40l. per annum. At prefent, the *net*

profits

profits upon this article, and upon
Sugar in Jamaica, are nearly equal per
acre; that is, 10 l. or 12 l. fterling.

In the year 1752, the export of
Coffee from Jamaica was rated at
60,000 pounds weight. In 1775, it
was 440,000 pounds. — Under the
prefent duty of fix pence per pound,
there is reafon to expect, that the ex-
ports may rather increafe than diminifh. But it is not likely to become a
fubject of very extenfive culture in
our Weft Indian Iflands, until even
this duty is lowered, or at leaft while
foreign Coffee is permitted to enter
into completion with it at the Britifh
market. Though the Planters of Jamaica, after a multitude of experi-

b 2 ments,

ments, and the moſt laudable exertions, have diſcovered the art of cultivating, picking, and curing the berries, ſo as to make their Coffee equal to the growth of Arabia; ſome ſamples have been produced from that Iſland, before the cultivation was ſo well underſtood as it is at preſent, which were pronounced, by the London dealers, even ſuperior to the beſt brought from the Eaſt.

" Two of the ſamples were equal
" to the beſt Mocha Coffee, and two
" more of them ſuperior to any Coffee
" to be had at the grocers ſhops in
" London, unleſs you will pay the
" price of *picked* Coffee for it, which
" is two ſhillings per pound more than
" for that which they call the beſt
" Coffee.

" Coffee. All the reft of the famples
" were far from bad Coffee, and very
" little inferior, if at all, to what the
" grocers call *beft* Coffee *."

WHAT revolutions may change the
nature of our commerce, were it poffible to forefee, it is not in my province
to examine; but the Legiflature of
England, as well as thofe of her Colonies, have had a wife example before
them, in the conduct of France, by
her promoting and protecting the
growth of every thing, that could fupply the place of articles which Europe purchafes in the Eaft Indies.
Piementa, or *Pimento (Myrtus Arborea
Aromatica foliis laurinis*), or All-fpice,

* Mr. *Stephen Fuller's* Letter to the Committee
of Correfpondence in Jamaica, dated, London, 28th
July, 1783.

as it is commonly called, from having a flavour compofed, as it were, of cloves, cinnamon, juniper berries, nutmegs, and pepper, is the peculiar fpice of Jamaica *: and it equals in virtues, and is more applicable to the general purpofes of life, and luxury too, than any fpice that is brought from the Eaft. The various ufes into which *Pimento* is converted in Europe, are but little known to thofe who raife it. One fecret, at leaft, I am able to divulge to them, which is, that its effential oil, coloured with *Alkanet Root*, to give it the appearance of

---

* From 12,000 to 15,000 bags of Pimento have been annually imported into England from Jamaica: each bag contains about one hundred weight. It pays a duty of about two pence per pound.

age,

age, is fold all over Europe for the oil of cloves *.

Sir Hans Sloane, in the Phil. Tranf. Abr. vol. II. p. 667. fays, that " *Piementa* may defervedly be counted the beft and moft temperate, mild, and innocent, of common fpices, and fit to come into greater ufe, and gain more ground, than it yet hath, of the Eaft India commodities of this kind; almoft all of which it far fur-paffes, by promoting the digeftion of meat, attenuating tough humours, moderately heating, ftrengthening the

* The principal and prevailing flavour of Pi-mento is like that of cloves: its oil exactly refem-bles the oil of that fpice, and finks as that does in water. The oil refides chiefly, like that of cloves, in the fhell, or cortical part.

fto-

ftomach, expelling wind, and doing thofe friendly offices to the bowels, we generally expect from fpices."

To this inferiority of the dear-bought and far-fetched fpices of the Eaft, I can bear ample teftimony;—and it ought further to be confidered, that the fpice in queftion, being the produce of one of our own Colonies, and growing there in the greateft abundance, can be afforded at a price that the poor of Great Britain may have all the comforts of its excellent properties; which I hope to have lei-fure to make fufficiently known to them hereafter.

THE

THE encouraging every article which increafes the intercourfe with our Colonies, is increafing our commerce. The payment for all the ftaples of the Weft Indies is made in our manufactures; the fale of which muft increafe in proportion to the numbers that are employed in the cultivation of what is bartered for them. Our Weft Indian Iflands, without draining us of fpecie or bullion, can fupply us with many of thofe very articles for which we are drained in other parts of the world *. The quantity of fhipping and feamen, neceffarily employed in

* The India Company pay for the Mocha Coffee in fpecie. The original coft is about 7 l. fterling per cwt.

carrying

carrying fupplies thither, and tranf-
porting their commodities back to Europe, muft be very confiderable. To
thefe reflections it muft alfo be added,
that the political difadvantage of not
encouraging our own Colonies is, that
we muft encourage thofe of other
countries, which have long fupplied
our markets, to the detriment of our
revenue, and the impoverifhing our
Colonies.

How long our fuperiority in fome
branches of manufacture may continue
to be the fource of wealth they are at
prefent, is uncertain; but by improving
the produce of our own foil, and encouraging the confumption at home,
of fuch commodities as give employment

ment to our own fubjects abroad, England will enrich her Colonies, and draw proportionate advantages; fecure their attachment, and eftablifh a population there, indifpenfable for the protection of thofe poffeffions, which are productive of the moft valuable and permanent commerce of the empire.

London, *Pall Mall*;
30 January, 1792.

A TREA-

TREATISE, &c.

IT is a generally received opinion, that the human frame is not lefs influenced by diet than by climate; that its difpofitions and characteriftics owe their originality as much to food, as thofe difeafes, evidently do, which are the legitimate and indifputable iffue of it.

IF the preceding pofition be juft, there cannot furely be a fubject more interefting to man, than the purfuit of that knowledge which may inftruct him to avoid what is hurtful to health, to felect for his ufe fuch things as tend to raife the value of his con-dition, and to carry the enjoyments of life totheir utmoft improvement.

WITH

With this idea, I submit to the public some obfervations which have occurred to me, on the dietetic and medicinal properties and effects of Coffee.

In England, the ufe of this berry hitherto has been principally confined to the occafional luxury of individuals; as fuch, it is fcarcely an object of public concern; but government, prudently confidering that this produce of our own Weft Indian Iflands is raifed by our own countrymen, and paid for in our manu-factures, has lately reduced the duty on the importation of Plantation Coffee; which has brought it within the reach of almoft every defcription of people *: and as it is not liable to any pernicious procefs in curing, and is incapable of adulteration, the ufe of it will probably become greatly ex-tended;—as in other countries, it may diffufe itfelf among the mafs of the people, and make a confiderable ingredient in their daily fuftenance.

* Good Plantation Coffee, roafted, may now be bought in London for two fhillings and fix pence per pound. In Paris the beft Martinico Coffee, roafted, may be bought for one fhilling and four pence per pound.

The

THE plant, the berries, and the beverage made from them, commonly pass under the same name. The Arabians, indeed, distinguish the trees and the berries by the name *Buun, Bunna, Buna,* and *Ban.*

THE beverage, of which we speak in particular, is called by the Egyptians *Eltave*; by the Persians *Cahwa,* and *Coho*; by the Turks *Chaube,* and *Cahveh*; by the Arabians *Cachua, Caoua,* and *Cahouah*; from whence originate *Caphé, Café, Coffi, Coffee,* and *Coffea,* appellations by which it is universally known in Europe.

THESE names, from the original Arabic, acquire the pronunciation they receive, by changing the *u* into *f,* in the word *Cahouah*; which, according to some writers, comes from a verb signifying to nauseate, or to have no appetite : and is one of the names which the Arabians give to wine, because it takes away the appetite, when drunk to excess.

THUS *Cahouah* they suppose is derived from the Hebrew קי, or קי, or קהי, which signify to have an aversion, or a dislike to a
b 8   thing.

thing. But *Golius, Meninſki,* and *Caſtel,* ſay, that *Cahouah* ſignifies to give an appetite, *quod appetentiam cibi adducit.* In oppoſition to both theſe opinions, there are others who aſſert, that *Cahouah* implies neither to give appetite, nor to take it away; and that it is not derived from the above words, importing to have, or to give diſtaſte, but from קוה, which ſignifies to give vigour and force,— *corroborare, roborare, confirmare*; and that *Cahouah* in Arabic means nothing more than to ſtrengthen, and to give vigour.

It is not impoſſible, notwithſtanding theſe opinions ſo plauſibly founded, but that this beverage might have its name from *Cufa* or *Cafa,* a city in Arabia Felix.

The Arabic *Ban* (the Coffee berry) correſponds with our *Bean,* and is probably its etymon. Perhaps the Greek Βύνη, "Barley ſteeped in water," Anglicè, *Malt,* may be traced from the Arabic *Buna.*

Numerous and abſurd have been the writers on *Coffee.* I have omitted to mention many; and of thoſe I have not, I hope it will be underſtood, that I have introduced them

to

to illuftrate opinions rather than fanction them.

THE botanical defcription of the *Coffee Plant* has been already given by feveral wri-ters*; and as Sir Hans Sloane, in the Phil. Tranf. N° 208, p. 63., Dr. Browne, in his Natural Hiftory of Jamaica, and Mr. Ellis, in 1774, have added to the number, it is unneceffary here to fay any thing on this part of the fubject, or to treat of its culti-vation; but I thought it might not be un-interefting in this Effay to include fomething

* *Bon. Alpin. De Plantis Ægypti*, cap. 16.

Bon vel Ban Arbor. J. Bauhin, 422.

Euonymo fimilis Ægyptiaca, fructu baccis Lauri fimili. C. Bauhin. Pinax. Theat. Botanic. 428.

Bon vel Ban ex cujus fructu Ægypti potum Coava conficiunt. Pluken. Phytog. 272.

Coffee frutex, ex cujus fructu fit potus. Raij Hiftor. Plant. t. 2. p. 1691.

Jafminum Arabicum cujus fructus Coffy dicuntur. Boerhaav. Ind. P. 2. p. 217.

Bon Arbor cum fructu fuo Buna. Parkinfon, Theatr. Botan. 1622.

Jaffaminum Arabicum, Lauri folio, cujus femen apud nos Café dicitur. Juffieu, Act. Gall. 1713, p. 388. t. 7.

Jafminum Arabicum, caftaneæ folio, flore albo odoratiffimo. Tilli Catal. Plant. Hort. Pifan. p. 87. t. 32.

Coffea Arabica, floribus quinquefidis difpermis. Linn. Spec. Plant. ed. 2. p. 245.

of

of its hiftory, which will shew it has been a topic of much difquifition, and no lefs remarkable for the univerfality with which it has been adopted by many regions of the Eaft, than for the permanency, after various perfecutions, with which it has been retained; notwithftanding the caprice of tafte, the violence of tyranny, and the aufterity of religion.

THE firft European who mentions Coffee, is in general underftood to be *Profper Alpinus*, who went into Egypt in 1580, phyfician to a Venetian Conful, and remained there three years.

IN 1592 he publifhed, in Venice, his Hiftory of the Plants of Egypt; wherein he gives an account of a tree, the feeds of which, called *Bon*, and *Ban*, were by decoction converted into a drink, much ufed by the Egyptians and Arabs. The great virtues of this liquor he alfo defcribes*.

BUT I muft obferve that, in the year 1591, *P. Alpinus*, immediately on his return, pub-

* De Plantis Ægypti, cap. 16.

lifhed

lifhed his *Medicina Ægyptiorum*, in which
he gave nearly the fame account of the tree
as in the preceding, which was a fubfequent
work; and here alfo he gave a very exact
defcription of the mode, ufed in Egypt, of
preparing the drink called *Chaoua*, from the
feeds of this tree, called *Bon*, and alfo from
their *capfules*. He is alfo particular as to the
different qualities of thefe two liquors, and
of the medicinal virtues of that, prepared
from the feeds *. The account given in this
work has been overlooked by almoft every
writer on Coffee. However, even with this
correction of common error, I find *Leonhart
Rauwolff*, a German phyfician, who had tra-
veled into the Eaft, has taken notice, though
not in an accurate manner, of Coffee as early
as 1573.

HE fays, at Aleppo, " They have a very
pleafant drink, called *Chaube*, which is almoft
as black as ink. It is good for illnefs, chiefly
that of the ftomach. It is made of a fruit called
Bunnu, which in bignefs, fhape, and colour,
refembles a bay berry. It is furrounded with

* De Medicina Ægyptiorum, Lib. IV. cap. 3.

C 2   two

two thin shells; and, as I was informed, is brought from the Indies. These shells have within them two yellowish grains, in two distinct cells, and agree in their virtue, figure, appearance, and name, with the *Bunchum* of *Avicenna*, and the *Bancha* of *Rhasis*; therefore I shall consider them to be the same, until I am better informed by the learned."

Of this opinion was *Faustus Naironus Bainesius*, who wrote the first treatise that was written expressly on Coffee. It was printed at Rome in 1671, and intituled, *De Saluberrima Potione Cahu, seu Cafe, nuncupata.*

Velschius, in his treatise *De Vena Medinensi*, in 1674, says, that the *Bunchum* of the Arabians is not Coffee, but the *Narcaphthum* of *Diascorides*.

In this *Velschius* is mistaken, and has no authority for the supposition, whether the *Bunchum* of *Avicenna* be Coffee or not.

The Νάρκαφθον of *Diascorides* is called by the Arabians *Nabach*; what it is, is uncertain;

3   tain;

tain; many are the conjectures; but *Dioscorides* mentions its use only for external purposes. Lib. I. cap. 22.

Avicenna's words respecting *Bunchum* are; " It is brought from *Yemen*; some say it is from the roots of *Amgailem*, which, when old (or *shaken*), falls down. The best sort is cream-coloured, and of a light grateful odour. The white and heavy (or *rank*), is not good. It is, according to some, hot and dry in the first degree; and to others, it is cold in the first degree. It strengthens the limbs, cleanses the skin, and dries up the watery humours; gives an agreeable odour to the body, prevents the hair from falling, and is good for the stomach." Lib. II. Tract. 2. cap. 91.

The *Ben* of *Avicenna* also has been supposed by some writers to be Coffee. *Prosper Alpinus* was of this opinion. But this is certainly an error.

Avicenna says of *Ben*, " The seed is larger than the cicer, inclining to whiteness, and has a soft unctuous pulp. It is hot in the third degree, and dry in the second. It is mundificative, particularly the pulp, and incites gross humours; with vinegar and water, it

opens

opens obstructions of the viscera. Externally, it is good for eruptions; in an emplaster, for all indurated abscesses, warts, &c.; with vinegar, for ulcerations, excoriations, scald head, &c. It is bad for the stomach, and causes nausea, and if taken with honey, excites vomiting and purging." Lib. II. Tract. 2. cap. 82.

Notwithstanding *P. Alpinus's* two publications, it appears that Coffee could have been but little known in Italy, when his countryman *Pietro Della Valle* was at Constantinople in 1615 *.

Mons. Du Four, who wrote on Coffee in 1685, says, the French knew nothing of it until 1645; and that it had not been used in France until about 1657. Monf. *Galland* also says, that its use was not known in France until Monf. *Thevenot* returned from his first voyage to the East in 1657, when he constantly

* " Hanno i Turchi un' altra bevanda di color nero; e la state si fà rinfrescativa, e l'inuerno al contrario, &c.— Ma senza queste dilicature ancora, co'l solo e semplice *Cahue*, è pur grata al gusto, e, come dicono, conferisce molto alla sanità; massimamente in aiutar la degestione; corroborar lo stomaco, e reprimer le flussioni de' catarri, &c.—Quando io farò di ritorno ne porterò meco; e farò conoscere all' Italia questo semplice, che infin' ad hora forse le è nuovo." Viaggi di *P. D. Valle*, Lettera 3.

5   drank

drank it, and treated his friends with it, at his houfe in Paris.

Mons. la Roque, who publifhed his Journey into Arabia Felix in 1715, confeffes, that *Thevenot* was the firft that taught the French the ufe of Coffee in 1657; but he contends, that his own father, having been with Monf. *De la Haye*, the French ambaf- fador at Conftantinople, and afterwards tra- veled in the Levant, did, when he returned to Marfeilles in 1644, drink Coffee every day; and brought with him not only Coffee, but all the little implements ufed in Turkey in pre- paring it. He fays alfo, that there was a public Coffee-houfe opened at Marfeilles in 1671, which was looked on as a great curiofity in France.

He fays, Coffee had fcarcely been feen in Paris before 1669; nor even heard of until that year, except in the houfe of *Thevenot*, and by the report of travellers.

In this year, *Solyman Aga*, Ambaffador from *Mahomet* the IVth came to Paris; and it is to this embaffy, *la Roque* fays, that the

firſt uſe of Coffee in Paris is to be attributed.

THIS embaſſy, which had given the Pari-
fians a general taſte for Coffee, and the method of making it, gave them alſo the idea
of public Coffee-houſes; for, in 1672, one
Paſcal, an Armenian, ſold it publicly at
the *Foire St. Germain*; and afterwards, in
the ſame year, opened a Coffee-houſe on the
Quai de l'Ecole, which was the firſt public
Coffee-houſe ever known in Paris.

COFFEE, however, was known in general
to the Engliſh before it was to the French or
Italians; and was uſed in England before
it was in France or Italy.

THE *Journal des Scavans*, 28th January,
1675, obſerves, " *les Anglais ont connu le
Café vingt ans plutôt que nous:* " and it appears, that theſe journaliſts were conſiderably
within the time, as far as relates to its having
been firſt noticed, by the travellers of the
reſpective countries.

WILLIAM FINCH, an Engliſh merchant, employed in the ſervice of the Eaſt-India Company

pany in 1607, fays, " That the people in the Ifland of *Socotora* have, for their beft entertainment, a China difh of *Coho*, a black bitterifh drink, made of a berry like a bay berry, brought from *Mecca*, fupped off hot; and it is reckoned good for the head and ftomach *."

But I am not certain whether *Biddulph's* account of the ufe of Coffee in the Eaft was not prior to *Finch's*. In a letter from him at Aleppo, which muft have been foon after the death of Queen Elizabeth in 1603, as he mentions that event as recent; he fays, " The Turks have for their moft common drink *Coffa*, which is a black kind of drink, made of a kind of pulfe like peas, called *Coava*; which being ground in a mill, and boiled in water, they drink it as hot as they can fuffer it, which they find to agree with them againft their crudities, and feeding on herbs, and raw meat. It is more wholefome than toothfome, for it caufeth a good concoction, and driveth away drowfinefs †."

* Purchas, p. 419.
† Ibid. p. 1340. See alfo p. 1351. where it appears that *Biddulph* was in the Eaft in 1600.

It

It is remarkable, that none of the travellers to the East, of any country, who have given the firft accounts of Coffee, have ever mentioned the circumftance on which all its virtues depend, — its torrefaction.

Having fhewn that the firft Coffee-houfe in Paris was opened in 1672, I now obferve, that the firft Coffee-houfe in London was opened in 1652.

Mr. Daniel Edwards, a Turkey merchant, when he returned from Smyrna to London in 1652, brought over with him a fervant, named *Pafqua Roffée*, a Ragufian Greek. This man ufed to prepare Coffee for him every morning, for his breakfaft. The novelty of this new repaft brought fo many people to Mr. *Edwards's* houfe, that he loft all the fore-part of the day in entertaining and fatisfying the curiofity of his vifitors. Thus fituated, he thought of an expedient to rid himfelf of the trouble, and to gratify his friends; which was, to fuffer his fervant to make and fell Coffee publicly. In confequence of which, *Pafqua* opened an

houfe

houfe in St. Michael's Alley, Cornhill, which was the firft Coffee-houfe in London *.

In 1660 (12 Car. II. cap. 24.) there was a duty of four pence per gallon laid on Coffee made and fold, to be paid by the maker; and in 1663 (15 Car. II. cap. 9. fect. 15.) all Coffee-houfes were licenfed at the general Quarter Seffions of the Peace for the County in which they were kept.

The following account is defcriptive of the commotions and prejudices which Coffee formerly had to contend with and conquer among the Mahometans. Befides the fimilitude it bears to the ludicrous notions, and contradictory opinions, concerning Coffee in later times, it may not be unentertaining to thofe who are accuftomed to reflect, how great communities are often violently agi-

* On the fpot, before the fire of 1666, where the Virginia Coffee-houfe now ftands. The firft Coffee-houfe that was opened after the fire was, what is now called Garraway's.

tated

tated by trifles; and that nations, under weak or oppreffive governments, as well as individuals, may be ferioufly ridiculous, and equally fubject to tranfitory delufion. It will appear alfo, that Coffee, which after many ftruggles triumphed over the fcrutiny of phyficians, had nearly funk under the influence of the *Alcoran*; but that the conteft between the *Alcoran* and Coffee ended, as it were, in a coalition.

"KHAIR BEG, Governor of *Mecca*, by appointment of the *Sultan* of Egypt, was unacquainted with Coffee, or of the manner of taking it. As he was going out of the Mofque one day, after evening prayer, he obferved in a corner of it a company of people drinking Coffee, who were to fpend the night there in prayer, and was much offended at it. He thought at firft they had been drinking wine; nor was his furprize much diminifhed after they had explained to him the ufe and virtues of this liquor. On the contrary, after they had informed him how much it was in ufe in *Mecca*, and what merriment paffed at the public places where it was fold, he was of opinion that Coffee

was

was intoxicating, at leaſt that it conduced to things forbidden by the law.

" For this reaſon, after having ordered theſe people to go out of the Moſque, with an injunction never to meet there for the future upon the like occaſion, he next day convened a great aſſembly of Officers of Juſtice, and Doctors of Law, together with Prieſts, and the moſt eminent men of *Mecca*; to whom he communicated what he had obſerved the night before in the Moſque, and what he was informed happened frequently in the public Coffee-houſes; adding, that he was reſolved to remedy this abuſe, upon which he was deſirous firſt to know their opinions.

" The Doctors agreed that the public Coffee-houſes wanted regulation, as being contrary to the law of pure Mahometiſm; and declared, that, with reſpect to Coffee, it was neceſſary to examine whether it was hurtful either to body or mind; and concluded to take the advice of phyſicians.

" The

" The Governor called in two Perfians who were brothers, the moft celebrated phyficians in *Mecca:* one of them even wrote againft the ufe of Coffee, jealous, perhaps, (fays our author) left the ufe of it fhould fpoil his practice; fo they did not fail to declare, that Coffee was cold and dry, and prejudicial to health.

" A DOCTOR of the affembly replied, That BENGIAZLAH *, an ancient Arabian phyfician of great authority, had faid, that thefe berries were hot and dry, and confequently could not have the qualities juft now afcribed to them.

" THE two Perfian phyficians replied, That BENGIAZLAH was a perfect ftranger to the berries in queftion; and declared, that if Coffee was reckoned among things indifferent, and free for every body to make ufe of, yet it was apt to lead to things not allowed of; and the fafeft way for true Muffulmen would be, to hold it unlawful.

* A celebrated phyfician of *Bagdat.* He died anno 1098.

" THIS

" THIS determination obtained all their
fuffrages; and feveral, either out of preju-
dice or falfe zeal, did not fail to affirm that
Coffee had actually difturbed their brains.
One of the affiftants maintained, that it intoxicated like wine, which fet all the affembly a laughing ; becaufe, in order to make a
judgment of it, it was neceffary to have
drunk wine, which is forbidden by the Mahometan religion. He was afked whether
he had ever drunk any wine ? and he had the
imprudence to anfwer in the affirmative;
which confeffion condemned him to the
baftinado, the punifhment that is inflicted by
the Mahometan law for this crime.

" COFFEE was, however, folemnly condemned at *Mecca*, as a thing forbidden by
law, notwithftanding the *Mufti* oppofed the
determination.

" The lovers of Coffee thought the fen-
tence would not hold water, as the *Mufti*
did not fign it, and even determined to pay
no regard to it in private. However, one of
them was furprized in the fact, and was
bafti-

7

baftinadoed, and was afterwards led about the city on an afs,

"But this rigour was not of long duration; for the *Sultan* of Egypt, far from approving of the indifcreet zeal of the Governor of *Mecca*, was fuprized that he fhould dare to condemn a thing fo much in favour at *Cairo*, the capital of his dominions, where there were Doctors of much greater authority than thofe of *Mecca*, and who had not found any thing in the ufe of Coffee contrary to the law.

"The *Sultan* ordered him therefore to revoke his prohibition, and to employ his authority againft the diforders only, if there were any, committed in the Coffee-houfes; adding, that becaufe *it was poffible to abufe the very beft things*, even the water of the fountain ZEMZEM *, in the Temple of MECCA, fo much efteemed by all Muffulmen, it was not for that reafon neceffary abfolutely to forbid them.

* The Mahometans fay this is the fpring that God caufed to iffue forth in the Defart for *Agar* and her fon *Ifhmael*, when *Abraham* fent them away.

"THE

" THE Governor was difplaced, and the two phyficians who bore a great part in the prohibition of Coffee, came to an unfortunate end.

" AFTER the re-eftablifhment of Coffee at *Mecca*, it was prohibited again, and again re-eftablifhed.

" THE *Sultan* of Egypt confulted his Doctors of the Law at Cairo upon this point; who gave their opinions in writing, and proved by fubftantial reafons, the fallacy of the condemnation of Coffee, and the ignorance of thofe who paffed it; which eftablifhed the ufe of Coffee at *Cairo*, upon a much ftronger footing than ever. But, in the end, this great city alfo met with much trouble upon the fubject. For, —

" IN the year 1523, a fcrupulous Doctor ftated, that Coffee intoxicated the head, and was prejudicial to health : and he had fufpicions that it was unlawful. But none of his brethren were of his opinion, becaufe it was obvious that Coffee had not thofe bad quali-

ties

ties he afcribed to it ; and therefore this gave
no fhock at all to a cuftom fo univerfally
received.

" But about ten years after, a preacher
held forth fo vehemently againft the ufe of
Coffee, as a thing prohibited by law, that the
mob fell upon the Coffee-houfes, broke the
pots and difhes, and abufed the company
they found there.

" Upon this, there were two parties formed
in the city ; one of which maintained that
Coffee was prohibited by law ; the other,
that it was not. But the Judge in Chief
having convened an affembly of all the
Doctors, to have their opinions, they
unanimoufly declared, that the queftion had
been already determined by their predeceffors
in favour of Coffee ; that they were all of
the fame fentiment ; and that there was nothing further neceffary than only to reftrain
the extravagant heat of the zealots, and the
indifcretion of ignorant preachers. The
Judge who prefided was of the fame opinion ; and immediately ordered all the affembly to be ferved with Coffee, and took fome

4   himfelf;

himfelf; an example which prefently compofed all controverfies, and made Coffee more
fafhionable at Cairo than before *."

THE commotions however which were
then excited by this beverage, were not confined to Mecca and Cairo; for *Pichevili*,
a Turkifh hiftorian, fays:

" AT the time when the ufe of Coffee was
moft prevalent in *Conftantinople*, the *Imams*
and officers of the Mofques made a great cla-
mour, that they were deferted, whilft all
the Coffee-houfes were continually crowded.
On which the Dervifes and Priefts made a
furious attack on Coffee; not only affirming
that it was unlawful, but that it was a much
greater fin to go to a Coffee-houfe than to a
Tavern.

" AFTER a great deal of noife and decla-
mation, all the Priefts united to obtain a fo-
lemn condemnation of this liquor; and
maintained that Coffee roafted was a fort of

---

* An Arabian manufcript, Nº 944, by *Abdalcader* of
Medina. It is in the great National Library at Paris;
written about the year 1587.

coal;

coal; and that every thing which had the
leaft relation to coal was forbidden by law.
Upon this they drew up a queftion in
form, and prefented it to the *Mufti*, with a
requeft that he would determine it according to the duty of his office. The *Mufti*,
without giving himfelf the trouble of examining any difficulties, gave a verdict
according to the wifh of the Priefts, and
pronounced that Coffee was prohibited by the
law of *Mahomet.*

" ALL the Coffee-houfes in *Conftantinople*
were immediately fhut up, and the officers
of the police ordered to prevent the drinking
Coffee in any manner whatever.

" YET, notwithftanding the rigour that
was employed in the execution of this order,
they could never prevent the drinking Coffee
in private: and *Amurath* III. in whofe time
this prohibition took place, again permitted
the ufe of it, in private houfes, and it grew
more and more into efteem. At laft, the
officers of the police, feeing there was no
remedy, were content, for a certain fum, to
permit

permit it to be fold in private houfes, fhutting up the doors, or in the back fhops.

" THERE wanted but little encouragement to re-eftablifh by degrees the public Coffee-houfes; and it happened that a new *Mufti*, lefs fcrupulous, or more wife, than his pre-deceffor, declared folemnly, that Coffee ought not to be looked upon as a coal; and that the liquor made from it was not prohibited by the law. After this declaration, the Zealots, Preachers, Doctors, and Lawyers, far from exclaiming againft Coffee, took it them-felves; and their example was univerfally followed by the whole Court and City."

COFFEE, though a native of *Arabia Felix*, is faid to have been converted into ufe in Africa and Perfia, long before a beverage was made of it by the Arabians.

OF the firft difcovery of the properties of Coffee there is no authentic account, that has come to the knowledge of European enquirers. But as fiction in fuch cafes generally fupplies the place of facts, it is impoffible that fo

d 3

im-

important an article as this in queftion fhould be deftitute of introductory anecdotes, on its firft appearance in the world.

FAUSTUS NAIRO, a native of the Holy-land, before-mentioned, who was Oriental Linguift in the College at Rome, and fome other romantic writers I have been under the neceffity of reading, pretend, that the extraordinary virtues of Coffee-berries were difcovered in nearly the following man-ner :

IN the nation of *Yemen*, a keeper of goats was one night much furprized that his herd would not go to fleep as ufual, but jumped and frifked about as if they had been infatuated. The next morning he went to *Sciadli*, the Prieft of the neighbouring Mofque, to intreat that he would inform him of the caufe of this wonderful change in the animals. The prieft defired the goatherd would conduct him to the pafture where they had fed on the preceding day. When he came there, he found the place covered with certain fhrubs with berries on them, of which the goats had eaten. Thefe fhrubs and berries had always
been

been confidered among the wild and ufelefs productions of the earth. The Prieſt, however, having fatisfied himfelf that thefe berries -had effected the alteration in the goats, gathered fome, went home and boiled them in water, and drank of the liquor. When night came, he perceived he could not fleep, but began to dance and frifk about as the goats had done. He reported thefe circumftances to the neighbouring Priefts, who all declared, that a liquor from thefe berries, properly prepared, would be an excellent thing to keep the Dervifes awake, when their duty obliged them to pray after dinner. The experiment was tried, and continued with the utmoft fuccefs; and was alfo attended with great advantage to their health. From the report of thefe Dervifes, the ufe of Coffee foon fpread through other Afiatic nations; and *Sciadli* was ever after drunk as a toaft, in a cup of Coffee, before any devotion was entered on, among all the religious of the Eaft.

BUT, turning from this ludicrous tale to the Arabian manufcript before-mentioned, tranflated by Monf. *Galland*, we find,

d 4   that

that about the middle of the fifteenth century, *Gemaleddin*, the *Mufti* of Aden, a city
in Arabia Felix, travelling into Perfia, learnt
the ufe of Coffee there, and on his return introduced it to his countrymen : who had no
fooner adopted the drinking of this beverage,
than they entirely neglected an herb which
had been long in ufe among them, called *Cat*,
of which they made an infufion, and drank
it in the manner in which we now drink Tea.

This herb, called by the Arabians *Cat*,
is, I believe, the fame as our Tea; for
it varies but little from the name which *Tea*
has always borne in the Eaftern countries,
being called by the Chinefe *Cha* and *The*; by
the Japonnefe and Indians, *Tchia*, *Tfia*, and
Cha; and by the Perfians *Tzai* and *Cha*.

Leyl fays, that *Cha* is a Tartarian
word; that the plant Tea, is indigenous in
Tartary, and is there, and in all the Eaftern
nations, called *Cha*; and that the Chinefe
only, who live near the coaft, and traffic
with Europeans, call it *The*. It is alfo fuppofed to have been unknown in China, until
the incurfions of the Tartars.

It

It is from the preceding epoch, distinguished by *Gemaleddin* the *Mufti*, that any authentic account of the dietetic use of Coffee is derived. Enthusiasm indeed has carried some absurd admirers of this beverage so far into conjecture, as to trace marvellous stories of it back to the remotest ages; and to suppose it the *Jus Nigrum* of the Lacedæmonians *; *Abigail's* cup to *David*, which saved her husband *Nabal's* life †; and the *Nepenthe* ‡, which *Helen* received from an Egyptian, and celebrated by *Homer* as a soother of the mind, in the extremest state of anger, grief, and misfortune ||.

From Aden it spread its influence to Mecca, Cairo, Damascus, and Aleppo; and afterwards through all Arabia, and other parts of the Ottoman Empire, and arrived at Constantinople, from Syria, in the reign of *Solyman* the Great, in the year 1554;

* *Muraltus*. *Herbert's* Travels. *Sandy's* Travels. *Blunt's* Voyage.

† *Paschius*, an obscure writer at Leipsic, 1700.

‡ *Pietro della Valle*.

" Φάρμακον, κακῶν ἐπίληθον ἁπάντων." Odyss. Δ.

introduced

introduced by two perfons whofe names were *Schems* and *Hekin* ; one came from Damafcus, the other from Aleppo ; each opened a public Coffee-houfe in that city ; and about a century afterwards, as I have already obferved, it was adopted at London and Paris.

THE virtues of this chearful liquor, like, moral virtues under defpotifm, operated in Conftantinople to its detriment ; —by difpelling the torpitude brought on by their vicious exceffes, and recruiting their fpirits, funk by depravity of their habits, it introduced a difpofition among the Turks to exercife the underftanding ; —a crime in every government that tolerates nothing but filent obedience.

RYCAUT fays, that during the war in Candia, in the minority of *Mahomet* the IVth, when the Turkifh affairs were in a critical fituation, " the *Vifir Kupruli* fuppreffed the Coffee-houfes, though he permitted the Taverns ;" the former conducing to intellectual recreation, and fome fpeculations on the affairs of ftate, which the *Vifir* thought

thought would not bear examining. Thefe were objections from which the latter, as tending only to idlenefs and debauchery, was free. This ftupid edict appears to have had no other relative effect than to diminifh the revenue; for Coffee throve under this political, as well as it did under the former religious, perfecution.

However ridiculous it may appear at this time, Coffee had the fame folly to encounter foon after its introduction into England; and experienced the fame treatment under *Charles* the IId, that it met with in Turkey under an *Amurath* and a *Mahomet*: for having been found an encourager of focial meetings, Coffee-houfes were fhut up by proclamation, as feminaries of fedition *.

This famous proclamation was dated 29th of December, 1675, and afferted that, " Becaufe in fuch houfes, and by occafion of the meeting of difaffected perfons in them, divers falfe, malicious, and fcandalous reports were devifed and fpread abroad, to the defamation of his *Majefty's government*, and to the dif-

* Anno 1675.

turbance

turbance of the quiet and peace of the realm."

THE opinion of the Judges was taken on this point, who in their great wisdom resolved, " That retailing of Coffee might be an innocent trade; but as it was used to nourish sedition, spread lies, and scandalize *great men*, it might also be a common nuisance."

RAY observed, that the part of Arabia which produced Coffee in such abundance, might truly be styled happy *; from whence many millions of bushels of this valuable treasure were then annually exported to Turkey, Barbary, and Europe +.—In Constantinople alone, the consumption is said to amount to more than what is expended for wine in Paris.

---

* The country of Yemen.

+ The Abbé *Raynal* says, that twelve millions five hundred and fifty thousand pounds weight of Coffee is annually exported from Arabia Felix; which, at 14 sols per pound, brings into that country 8,785,000 livres, 384,343 l. 15 s. sterling. The European Companies purchase three millions five hundred thousand weight of this commodity.

It

IT was long after Coffee had been an article of commerce, that Europeans were able to obtain, or cultivate, the plant; as the berry was exported dry, and unfit for propagation.

IT has been said, that a Frenchman, near *Dijon* in France, was the first person who made the experiment with success, about the year 1670: the trees raised from the seeds he had sown produced berries, but they were tastelefs and infipid; and served for no other purpose than curiosity.

ACCORDING to *Boerhaave's* account, a Dutch Governor was the first person who procured fresh berries from Mocha, and planted them in *Batavia*; and in the year 1690 sent a plant from thence to Amsterdam; which came to maturity, and produced those berries which have since furnished all that is now cultivated in the West Indies.

IN 1714 a plant, from the garden of Amsterdam, was sent by Mr. *Pancras*, a Burgomaster, and Director of the Botanic Garden,

Garden, as a prefent to *Lewis* the XIVth, which was placed in the garden at Marly.

In 1718 the Dutch began to cultivate Coffee in Surinam; in 1721 the French began to cultivate it at Cayenne; in 1727 at Martinico; and in 1728 the Englifh began to cultivate it in Jamaica.

M. FUSEE AUBLET, in his Obfervations on the Culture of Coffee, annexed to the ingenious Mouf. *Le Breton's* Paris tranflation of the third edition of this Treatife, fays that a Monf. *de Clieux* carried the firft Coffee plant to Martinico in 1720; and that the French Eaft-India Company fent fome plants to the Ifle of Bourbon in 1717; and that one plant only furvived, which bore in 1720, and many were produced from it.

THE firft plant in Jamaica was introduced by Sir *Nicholas Laws*, and planted at Townwell eftate, now called Temple Hall, in Liguanea, belonging to Mr. *Luttrell.*— How its propagation has been extended fince thofe periods, in the Weft Indies, is well known.

SOME

SOME writers imagine that there are several sorts of Coffee*; but the difference arises only from the soil, cultivation, curing, and keeping, and not from any difference in the species.

IF the Coffee in our West-Indian Islands be planted in a dry soil, and in a warm situation; if, after the trees have acquired a certain age, the ripe berries are collected with care and cleanliness, which will be small when dry, cream-coloured, and with a smooth polished surface, like those which come from Arabia; and if they are kept a proper time before they are used; this Coffee will have flavour and excellence equal to the best that is imported from Mocha.

BUT the time and labour necessary to produce Coffee of the best quality have discouraged our Planters from raising it at much expence; because, until lately, it has been subject to a precarious, or losing market. Therefore quantity, and large coarse berries

---

* *Geoffry*, among others, was mistaken in this point.

of a green dingy caſt, the produce of young
trees, luxuriant ſoil, and little attention, has
turned to better account than quality;
as this produce, though unfit for the
London market, has been bought up for
the conſumption of the Northern parts of
Europe *.

AFTER Coffee has received all the excellence it can from the Planter, it is a matter
of great conſequence, that proper care be
taken in ſhipping it for Europe: it ſhould
not be put into parts of the veſſel where it
may be injured by dampneſs, or by the
effluvia of other freight. Coffee-berries are
remarkably diſpoſed to imbibe exhalations
from other bodies, and thereby acquire an
adventitious and diſagreeable flavour. Rum
placed near to Coffee will in a ſhort time ſo
impregnate the berries, as to injure their
flavour. It is ſaid, that a few bags of pepper

* Mr. *Fuller* obſerves in his letter, " I would recom-
mend to the Planters, not to covet the production of the
large berries, the ſmalleſt being deemed the beſt by our
buyers here, and fetching the moſt money; perhaps not
abſolutely from its being of the beſt quality, but becauſe it
admits of being mixed with the Mocha Coffee, and ſold as
ſuch."

on board a ſhip from India, ſome years ſince, ſpoiled a whole cargo of Coffee *.

THE French are more attentive in this, reſpect than the Engliſh; and indeed they omit nothing that can give their Coffee any advantage. But if their Coffee be ſuperior to ours, it is the effect of more encouragement. The induſtry and genius of the French Coffee Planters have been cheriſhed; ours have been reſtricted by a duty, which prevented the conſumption of the article. Thus the ſpirit of cultivation has been checked, improvement retarded, and conſequently the produce not brought to perfection.

THE chemical analyſis of Coffee evinces that it poſſeſſes a great portion of mildly bitter, and lightly aſtringent gummous and reſinous extract †; a conſiderable quantity of oil ‡; a fixed ſalt ‖; and a volatile ſalt §.——
Theſe

---

* Mil'er.

† Newman obtained eight ounces from ſixteen ounces of roaſted Coffee, by aqueous and ſpirituous menſtruums.

‡ Bourdelin obtained ſix ounces ſix drams from two pounds and an half of roaſted Coffee: and Houghton, Phil.

Thefe are its medicinal conftituent principles.

THE intention of torrefaction is not only
to make it deliver thofe principles, and make
them foluble in water, but to give it a property it does not poffefs in the natural ftate of
the berry.

BY the action of fire, its leguminous tafte
and the aqueous part of its mucilage are de-
ftroyed; its faline properties are created, and
difengaged, and its oil is rendered empyreumatic. — From thence arifes the pungent
fmell, and exhilarating flavour, not found
in its natural ftate *.

Tranf. obtained two ounces four drams two fcruples from
one pound of unroafted Coffee. *Du Four* obtained two
ounces five drams.

|| *Le Fevre, Newman, Lemery, Bourdelin,* obtained nine
drams and an half from two pounds and an half of roafted
Coffee.

§ *Floyer, Bourdelin,* obtained a volatile falt, that effer-
vefced ftrongly with fpirit of falt.

* There always prevailed a notion among the chemifts,
particularly with *Paracelfus* and his followers, that in the
empyreumatic oils of plants were many medicinal virtues
undifcovered. The oil of Coffee, in itfelf, is almoft
infipid.

4   ANIMAL

ANIMAL oils are changed by fire in the same manner in broiled meats, and acquire that grateful odour fo exciting to weak appetites.

IMITATIONS of Coffee have been procured from roafted beans, peas, wheat, and rye, with almonds; but the delicacy of the oil in Coffee, which the fire, in roafting, converts into its peculiar empyreuma, is not to be equalled.

THE roafting of the berry to a proper degree, requires great nicety: *Du Four* juftly remarks, that the virtue and agreeablenefs of the drink depend on it, and that both are often injured in the ordinary method. *Bernier* fays, when he was at *Cairo*, where it is fo much ufed, he was affured by the beft judges, that there were only two people in that great city, in the public way, who underftood the preparing it in perfection *.

* *Bernier's* Letter to *Du Four*.

IF

If it be under-done, its virtues will not be imparted, and in ufe it will load and oppreſs the ſtomach : — If it be over-done, it will yield a flat, burnt, and bitter taſte, its virtues will be deſtroyed, and in ufe it will heat the body, and act as an aſtringent *.

Fourteen pounds weight of raw Coffee is generally reduced, at the pubic roaſting houfes in London, to eleven pounds by the roaſting ; for which the dealer pays feven pence half-penny, at the rate of five fhillings for every hundred weight. In Paris, the fame quantity is reduced to ten pounds and an half. But the roaſting ought to be regulated by the age and quality of the Coffee, and by nicer rules than the appearance of the fumes, and fuch as are ufually practiſed : therefore the reduction muſt confequently vary, and no exact ſtandard can be afcertained. Befides, by mixing different forts of Coffee together, that require different degrees of heat and roaſting, Coffee has feldom all

* " Cetera bonitas Caovæ præcipuè dependet à curiofa et exquiſita toſtione." *Ray.*

the

the advantages it is capable of receiving, to make it delicate, grateful, and pleasant. This indeed can be effected no way so well as by people who have it roasted in their own houses, to their own taste, and fresh as they want it for use.

The closer it is confined at the time of roasting, and till used, the better will its volatile pungency, flavour, and virtues, be preserved.

Coarse, rank, new Coffee, is meliorated by being kept after it is roasted, before it is used.

The influence which Coffee, judiciously prepared, imparts to the stomach, from its invigorating qualities, is strongly exemplified by the immediate effect produced on taking it, when the stomach is over-loaded with food, or nauseated with surfeit, or debilitated by intemperance, or languid from inanition.

To constitutionally weak stomachs, it affords a pleasing sensation; it accelerates the process of digestion, corrects crudi-

ties,

ties, and removes the cholic, and flatulencies.

BESIDES its effect on the gaſtric powers, it diffuſes a genial warmth that cheriſhes the animal ſpirits, and takes away the liſtleſsneſs and languor *, which ſo greatly embitter the hours of nervous people, after any deviation to exceſs, fatigue, or irregularity.

THE foundation of all the miſchiefs of intemperance is laid in the ſtomach ; when that is injured, inſtead of preparing the food, that the lacteals may carry into the conſtitution ſweet and wholeſome juices to the ſupport of health, it becomes the ſource of diſeaſe, and diſperſes through the whole frame the cauſe of decay.

FROM the warmth and efficacy of Coffee in attenuating the viſcid fluids, and increaſing the vigour of the circulation, it has been uſed with great ſucceſs in ſome caſes of fluor albus, and in the dropſy † ; and alſo in worm

* *Baglivi.*

† " C'eſt fans doute ſon fréquent uſage qui garentit les Turcs de l'hydropiſie." *Du Four*, p. 129.

complaints *;—and in thofe camatofe, ana-
farcous, and fuch other difeafes as arife from
unwholefome food, want of exercife, weak
fibres, and obftru&ed perfpiration.

In vertigo, lethargy, catarrh, and all
diforders of the head from obftru&ion in
the capillaries, long experience has proved it
to be a powerful medicine †; and in certain
cafes of apoplexy, it has been found ferviceable
able even when given in glyfters, where it
has not been convenient to convey its effe&s
by the ftomach. Monf. *Malebranche* reftored
a perfon from an apoplexy by repeated
glyfters of Coffee ‡.

* *Anthelminticum* audit, et hinc pueris fæpe confertur,
copiofius vero hauftum, parvos eos reddit, deoque non
facile his ordinandum. Si quis aliquot Cyathos deco&i
faturatioris hauriat, vermes plerumque e ventriculo in
inteftina defcendere experitur; fi mox purgatio propinetur,
invifi hi hofpites hac methodo expelluntur. *Linnai*,
Amœnitat. Academ. Vol. VI. p. 178.

† " La tête eft la partie de tout le corps fur laquelle le
Caffé produit de plus confidérables effets ; car par fon
ufage ordinaire, on prévient prefque fûrement l'apoplexie,
la paralyfie, la lethargie, et prefque toutes les autres
maladies foporeufes." *De Bleguy*, p. 180.

‡ Hift de l'Acad. de Sciences, 1702.

THERE are but few people who are not informed of its utility for the head-ach; the steam sometimes is very useful to mitigate pains of the head.

In the West Indies, where the violent species of head-ach, such as cephalæa, hemicrania, and clavus, are more frequent, and more severe than in Europe, Coffee is often the only medicine that gives relief. Opiates are sometimes used, but Coffee has an advantage that Opium does not possess; it may be taken in all conditions of the stomach; and at all times by women, who are most subject to these complaints; as it dissipates those congestions and obstructions that are frequently the cause of the disease, and which Opium is known to increase, when its temporary relief is past *.

* Ego cum Lugduni Batavorum studiis operam darem, per totum annum Cephalæa miserè laboravi; et postquam potui copiose Teé, et præcipuè quidem *Coffee* quotidie sumendo assuevi, semper immunis ab ea vixi, non tantúm sed ab omni alio incommodo, quamvis antea ita vixerim, ut mortis haberet vices lenta quæ trahebatur mihi vita gementi, qui per totum quinquennium cum longa morborum serie acriter conflictavi. *Ray.*

FROM

From the ſtimulant and detergent properties of Coffee, it may be uſed to an extent to
be ſerviceable in all obſtrucctions ariſing from
languid circulation. It aſſiſts the ſecretions,
promotes the menſes, and mitigates the pains
attendant on the ſparing diſcharge of that
evacuation.

In the Weſt Indies, the chloroſis and
obſtructed menſes are common among
laborious negro females, expoſed to the
effects of their own careleſſneſs, and the
rigorous tranſitions of the climate; there
ſtrong Coffee is often employed as a deob-
ſtruent; which, drank warm in a morning
faſting, and uſing exerciſe 'after it, has been
productive of many cures *. From its poſ-
ſeſſing

* " Utuntur tamen ejus decocto ad roborandum ventri-
culum frigidiorem, adjuvandamque concoctionem, et non
minùs ad auferendas a viſceribus obſtructiones; in tumo-
ribuſque hepatis lieniſque frigidis, et antiquis obſtruc-
tionibus, feliciori cum ſucceſſu decoctum multos dies expe-
riuntur. Quod etiam uterum maximè reſpicere videtur,
ipſum enim excalfacit, obſtructioneſque ab eo aufert, ſic
enim in familiari uſu eſt apud omnes Ægyptias, Arabaſ-
que mulieres, ut ſemper, dum fluunt menſes, ipſorum
vacuationem, hujus decocti ferventis multum paulatim
ſorbillantes, adjuvent. Ad promovendos etiam, in quibus ſuppreſſi ſunt, uſus hujus decocti, purgato corpore
multis

seſſing theſe qualities, *Geoffrey* cautions preg-
nant women, and ſuch as are ſubject to
exceſſive menſtruation, to uſe it in modera-
tion.

THE induſtrious overſeers of plantation's,
and other Europeans employed in cultivation
in the Weſt Indies, who are expoſed to the
morning and evening dews, find great ſupport from a cup of Coffee before they go into
the field : it fortifies the ſtomach, and guards
them againſt the diſeaſes incident to their
way of life; eſpecially in clearing lands ;
or when their reſidence is in humid ſituations,
or in the vicinity of ſtagnant water. Thoſe
who are imprudently addicted to intemperance find Coffee a benign reſtorer of the
ſtomach, for that nauſea, weakneſs, and
diſorderly condition, which is brought on by
drinking bad fermented liquors, and new rum,
to exceſs.

IN continued and remitting fevers in hot
climates, it frequently happens, at the period

multis diebus, utiliſſimus eſt." *P. Alpin.* Lib. de Plantis
Ægypti, cap. 16.——" Pellens eſt ; qua ratione, non ſine
fructu, tanquam emmenagogum, in menſtruis ſuppreſſis
adhibetur. *Linnæi*, Amœnitat. Acad. Vol. VI. p. 179.

when

when bark is indicated, that the ſtomach cannot retain it.—This is an embarraſſment of great importance, in which the practitioner has an interval, only of a few hours, to decide on his patient's fate.—Bark in ſubſtance is required to anſwer the intention; and here, as well as in many caſes of intermittents, when every other mode of adminiſtering bark has proved abortive, Coffee has been found an agreeable and a ſucceſsful vehicle.

In obſtinate intermittents, where a courſe of bark has been long continued, it ſeldom fails to increaſe thoſe viſceral obſtructions which are incidental to the diſeaſe itſelf.

To aſſiſt the bark in its operation, I have often uſed Coffee; and have known inſtances where it has removed ſlight intermittents; and for thoſe obſtructions, which the diſeaſe, or bark, or both, frequently leave after them, and which patients are often obliged to ſuffer, as the leaſt evacuation brings on a return of fever, I have alſo recommended Coffee, to make a conſiderable portion in the diet, with advantage.

CoFFEE

COFFEE having the property of promoting perfpiration *, it allays thirſt and checks preternatural heat.

Sir *John Chardin*, when in Perſia †, cured himſelf of a bloody flux by drinking four cups of hot Coffee, and going to bed, and covering himſelf well with bed clothes. But this cure was occaſioned by the perſpiration it produced; though he attributed it to ſome ſpecific quality in the Coffee.

THE great uſe of Coffee in France is ſuppoſed to have abated the prevalency of the gravel.—In the French Colonies, where Coffee is more uſed than in the Engliſh, as well as in Turkey, where it is the principal beverage, not only the gravel, but the gout, thoſe tormentors of ſo many of the human race, are ſcarcely known ‡.

TAVER-

---

* *Leewenhoek, Huxham.*

† Anno 1671.

‡ *Urinam* copioſe pellit, imprimis ſi aqua miſceatur; quoſdam calculo obnoxios Halmiæ novimus, qui cyathum Coffeæ murrhinum vitro aquæ frigidæ, libra una repleto, infundunt,

TAVERNIER fays, the Perfians are totally unacquainted with the gout and gravel ; and Monf. *Spon*, a celebrated Phyfician at Lyons, who had travelled in the Eaft, fays, thefe difeafes are rarely met with in the Levant, which they attribute to the great ufe of Coffee in thofe parts of the world. But climate, I apprehend, which the encomiafts of Coffee will not admit, ought to be taken into the account.

DU FOUR relates, as an extraordinary in-ftance of the effects of Coffee in the gout, the cafe of Monf. *Deverace*. He fays, this gentleman was attacked with the gout at twenty-five years of age, and had it feverely until he was upwards of fifty, with chalk ftones in the joints of his hands and feet; but for four years preceding, the account of his cafe being given to *Du Four*, to lay before the publick, he had been recommended the

infundunt, idque horis confumunt matutinis, qui unani-miter fatentur, qued vix aliud ipfis fit notum, urinam et fabulum copiofius pellens. *Linnæi*, Amœnitat. Acad. Vol. VI. p. 177.

ufe

ufe of Coffee, which he adopted, and had no return of the gout afterwards *.

COFFEE has been found ufeful in quieting the tickling vexatious cough that often accompanies the fmall pox †, and other eruptive fevers.—A difh of ftrong Coffee without milk or fugar, taken frequently in the paroxyfm of fome afthmas, abates the fit; and I have often known it to remove the fit entirely. Sir *John Floyer*, who had been afflicted with the afthma from the feventeenth year of his age until he was upwards fourfcore, found no remedy in all his elaborate refearches, until the latter part of his life, when he obtained it by Coffee.

PREPARED ftrong and clear, and fweetened agreeably with fugar-candy, and diluted, while hot, with a great portion of boiling milk, it becomes an highly nutritious and balfamic diet; proper in fuch hectic and pulmonic complaints, where a milk diet is

* " Elle eft falutaire aux goutteux par l'expérience particulière de nos goutteux, qui s'y font habitués : car ils en tirent du moins ce bénefice que leur accès font moins fréquent et beaucoup plus fupportables." *De Blegny*, p. 185. et 186.

† *Huxham.*

ufeful;

ufeful*; and is a great reftorative to conftitutions emaciated by the gout and other
chronic diforders †·

Nieuhoff, a German phyfician, in his account of the embaffy from Holland to China
in 1675, firft defcribed the advantage of milk
Coffee in pulmonic complaints.

Monf. *Monin,* an eminent phyfician of
Grenoble, performed many extraordinary
cures with it among confumptive people,
when a milk diet, affes milk, and the air of
Montpellier, had proved ineffectual. He relates the following cafe of his wife; of whom,
he fays,—" fhe had been in a confumption for
fixteen years, and was at the point of death
lately with a peripneumony. The inflam-
mation of the lungs was removed by the
ordinary methods in eight days; there re-

* " Elle eft d'un effet merveilleux pour ceux qui ont
la poitrine naturellement foible, ou accidentellement
affoiblie par le rheume, par le toux inveterée, par une
pulmonie naiffante, et par ces autres efpèces de fluxions
qui rendent la voix rauque, et qui caufent l'afthme et la
courte haleine." *De Blegny,* p. 189.

† This is the beft method of preparing *Milk Coffee.* It
may be fweetened with good Mufcovada fugar, in coftive
habits, or where fugar-candy cannot be had.

mained

mained a very troublefome cough, an heat in the lungs, and quick pulfe, with a great dryneſs of the ſkin, which made me apprehend ſhe would fall again into her confumptive ſtate. I prepared her by gentle purgatives and aperient medicines, as her bowels were in a bad ſtate, and her ſpleen obſtructed, and put her on a courſe of aſſes milk, which ſhe took regularly for a month, but without the leaſt ſuccefs; her pulfe remained the fame, her cough was worfe, ſhe ſpit more, her complexion was yellow, fometimes greeniſh; ſhe complained of heats, and oppreſſions of her breaſt, notwithſtanding the exact regimen, and gentle purgatives repeated every week. Finding that the aſſes milk was ufelefs, I again put her on a courſe of her former milk Coffee, of which ſhe took about a quart every day for ſix weeks, purging her every ten or twelve days. This courſe was ſo favourable to her, that all the ſymptoms beforemetioned ceafed in the firſt eight days; her appetite ſoon returned, and ſhe grew more *en bon point* than ſhe had ever been in her life."

LONG watching and intenfe ſtudy are wonderfully ſupported by it, and without
the

the ill confequences that fucceed the fufpenfion of reft and fleep, when the nervous
influence has nothing to fuftain it.

THEVENOT fays, " When merchants in
Turkey have any letters to write, and intend
to do it in the night-time, in the evening
they take a difh or two of Coffee, which is
good to hinder vapours, head-ach, and to take
away fleepinefs, &c.—In fhort, in the Turk's
opinion it is good againft all maladies, and
certainly it hath at leaft as much virtue as is
attributed to tea ; and as to its tafte, by that
time a man hath drank of it twice, he is
accuftomed to it, and finds it no longer un-
pleafant."

WE are told, that travellers in Eaftern
countries, and meffengers who are fent with
difpatches, perform their tedious journies by
the alternate effects of Opium and Coffee ;—
and that the dervifes and religious zealots, in
their abftemious devotions, fupport their
vigils, through their nocturnal ceremonies,
by this antifoporific liquor.

f   Du

Du FOUR fays, the poor people in Turkey ufe it through œconomy to fave victuals; as frequently two or three cups of Coffee is their whole fuftenance in the courfe of a day.

BERNIER fays, that the Turks, who frequently fubfift a confiderable time upon Coffee only, look on it as an aliment that affords great nourifhment to the body: for which reafon, during the rigid faft of the Ramadam, or Turkifh Lent, it is not only forbidden, but any perfon is deemed to have violated the injunctions of the Prophet, that has had even the fmell of Coffee*.

BACON fays, Coffee " comforts the head and heart, and helps digeftion †." Dr. *Willis*

* Nous remarquerons, qu'ayant fait ufage de cette boiffon, nous avons découvert qu'outre les qualités qu'on vient rapporter, elle a celle de foutenir les forces contre l'inanition, en forte qu'étant prife à jeun, on peut fe paffer plus long temps de nourriture, fans en être incommodé. *Journ. des Sc.* 1716, p. 283.

† Cent. 8, Exp. 738. anno 1624.—*Bacon* afferted this on the authority of travellers, as Coffee was not then known in England.

fays,

fays, " being daily drank, it wonderfully clears and enlightens each part of the foul, and difperfes all the clouds of every function *." The celebrated Dr. *Harvey* ufed it often. *Voltaire* lived almoft on it. He told me, nothing exhilarated his fpirits more than the fmell of Coffee; for which reafon he had, what he ufed in the day, roafted in his chamber every morning, when he lived at *Fernai*.—The learned and fedentary of every country have recourfe to it, to refrefh the brain, oppreffed by ftudy and contemplation †.

AMONG the many valuable qualities of Coffee, that of its being an antidote to the abufe of *Opium* muft not be confidered as the leaft; for as mankind is not content with the wonderful efficacy derived from the prudent ufe of opium, the abufe of it is productive of many evils that are only remediable by Coffee.

* Pharmaceut. Rat. P. 1. Anno 1674. Coffee was then ufed in England.

† " Elle fortifie la mémoire et le jugement. Un aliment qui fortifie puiffamment toutes les actions naturelles." *De Blegny*, p. 181. 184.

THE

THE difeafes generally brought on by a continued courfe of exceffive dofes of Opium, are either lofs of appetite, ftupor, debility, lofs of memory, melancholy, palfy, or dropfy:—and frequently the confequences of the neceffary and temporary ufe of common dofes of laudanum, are naufea, languor, giddinefs of the head, cold fweats, head-ach, hyfterics, and tremor.

VARIOUS have been the attempts of phyficians and chemifts to correct their favourite Opium, and to improve and feparate its ufeful from its hurtful properties *; but their preparations have neither meliorated the fimple juice of the vegetable, as the great *Sydenham* afferts, nor have they taken away thofe properties to which its prejudical effects are attributed.

THERE never has been, as far as we know, any preparation or combination with Opium,

* *Paracelfus, Helmont, Silvius*, and *Platerus.*—The ufe of Opium in the Lues Venerea is by no means a new difcovery, as fome practitioners have lately thought. It has had its advocates and ufe, like Guaiacum, and other diaphoretics. It was known to *Paracelfus, 'Fernilius, Palmarius, Willis, Paulli*, &c.

from

from the days of *Mithridates* to the prefent, that could be relied on, to coun-
teract the ill effects of its firft operations, in
many conftitutions; or to prevent thofe difa-
agreeable after-operations fo much complained
of, in almoft every fubject and difeafe.

Such a preparation would indeed be a
large contribution to the Materia Medica,
and would make a confiderable figure in the
practice of phyfic. But this may never be
accomplifhed; it may not be in nature; the
defect may be the inherent imperfection of
the vegetable, and infeparable from it;—as
in the moral world we find the brighteft
virtues may be fhaded with alloy:—if fo,
it will yet be fome confolation, that we are
able to mitigate thofe ills which we cannot
prevent.

Every author who mentions Coffee,
allows that it poffeffes fingular power in
counteracting the hypnotic, or fleepy effects
of Opium: this is the only virtue affigned
to it, in regard to Opium; as if the influence which Coffee exerts on the fyftem, to
produce that effect, could be directed to no

purpose, when these contradictions were not employed in opposition, to rob each other of their attributes.

Confirmed by many observations, I believe that Coffee, besides being the best corrector of Opium, is the best medicine to alleviate the mischief it produces, that has yet been discovered, and that the operations of common doses of Opium may be checked by it almost at pleasure.

The heaviness, head-ach, giddiness, sickness, and nervous affections, which attack the patient in the morning, who has taken an opiate at night, are abated by a cup or two of strong Coffee.

In Military Hospitals in hot climates, recourse is often had to large and repeated doses of Opium; from which I have frequently observed, that the retention of the stomach of the patient has been greatly injured; the secretion of urine impeded, or the bladder affected by a paralysis:— even these effects have been subdued by a few cups of strong Coffee.

THE

THE general opinion is erroneous, though of long standing, that the *Turks* use Coffee, exclusive of dietetic purposes, only against the sleepy effects of Opium.

The *Turks*, as well as the *Persians* and *Indians*, take Opium as a cordial *, to invigorate them for the temporary enjoyment of amorous pleasures, and to enable them to support fatigue, and to stimulate their nerves to the exertions of courage and enterprize †. But when the desired effects of this cordial are over, languor, lassitude, and dejection of spirits succeed. — It is for these indispositions, that Coffee is so medicinally necessary to the *Turks*, and they use it as their principal remedy.

* "Præstantissimum sit remedium cardiacum, unicum penè dixerim, quod in natura hactenus est repertum." *Sydenham*.

† *Mandelslo's* Voyages and Travels into the East, Lib. I. *Bellonius*, Lib. III. cap. 15. *Erastus*, Disp. de Sapor. et de Narcot. *Georg. Andreæ*, Itiner. Ind. Lib. II. c. 9. *J. J. Saar*. Itiner. Ind. p. 11. *Fogelius* de Turcarum Nepenthe. *Sandy's* Travels, Lib. I. p. 66.

BUT

But while this unpleasing review of Opium is presented to our contemplation, let us not forget the benefit which mankind derives from that inestimable medicine.

If the *Silphium* was held in veneration, stamped on coins, and hung up in temples *; if the *Mallow* was dignified with the name of Sacred †; if a statue was erected to the *Lettuce* ‡;— what honours are not due to the Poppy, whose pure and unadulterated juice possesses power to relax the whole force of animal spasm; to arrest the determination of the fluids and vital energy on particular parts, which often tends to the sudden dissolution of the frame; to relieve corporal pain by tranquillity, and mental affliction by sleep §. These are the unrivalled virtues of the Poppy, so highly distinguished by the

---

* *Plin. Hist. Nat.* Lib. XIX. c. 3. *Hefchius*, Βάτιυ σίλφιον. *Spanheim*, de usu et præst. Numis. Differt. 4.

† By *Pythagoras.*

‡ By *Augustus.* Several of the *Valerian* family ennobled their name with that of *Lactucinii. Plin.*

§ " Tam homini quam morbo conciliat." *Paracel.*

Creator,

Creator, and whofe excellence no human praife can reach.

It is not to be expected that Coffee fhould efcape objections, when the virtues of Opium could not fecure that from cenfure and con-demnation. Among the furious enemies of Opium was Profeffor *Stahl*, of Hall in Germany *; and among thofe of Coffee was *Simon Paulli* of Roftock. As the former could fee nothing but the mifchiefs of Opium, fo the latter was blind to the virtues of Coffee. But *Paulli* founded his prejudices againft Coffee, as he had his pre-judices againft Tea, Chocolate, and Sugar— not on experience, but on anecdotes, that had been picked up by hafty travellers, which had no other foundation than abfurd report and conjecture †. Unacquainted with the real properties of Coffee, his imagination fupplied him with fictitious ones; and claffed with articles with which it has no more affinity than they have analogy to each

* De Opij Impoftura.
† *Olearius, Martinius, Garranciers,* &c.

other *,

other *, he affigned to it thofe qualities which fhould affect the body, according to fome theory of *Galen* which had mifled him, to correfpond with the account he had read of its fuppofed effects on Sultan *Mahomet Cafnin*, a defpot of Perfia ; who, it is faid, from an exceffive fondnefs of Coffee, had fotted away the vigour of his conftitution †. But chemiftry and experience have brought the fubject into light, and *Paulli's* bafelefs fabric has vanifhed.

SUCH has been the fate of *Fernelius's* declamations againft mercury ; fuch *Guy Patin's* againft antimony ; and fuch *James* the Firft's, and the Abbot *Niffens's* nonfenfe againft tobacco ‡.

* " Inflar Rutæ, Agni Cafti, Camphoræ, Theè, Coffee, Chocoladæ, et fimilium omnis," &c. *S. Paulli*, Quadrip. Botan. p. 396.

† This ftory is related in the Travels of the Ambaffadors from the Duke of Holftein into *Mufcovy* and *Perfia*, Lib. VI. It originated from a complaint made againft *Cafnin* by his wife. This lady was of a different opinion from the Marquis *de Langle*, who, in his *Voyage en Efpagne*, fays,—" Le Caffé égaye, exalte, électrife ; à l'homme qui a pris du Caffé en abondance, il ne manque plus qu'une femme, une plume, et l'encre."

‡ The Abbot *Niffens* maintained, that the Devil firft brought tobacco into Europe.

I HAVE

I HAVE fingled out *Simon Paulli* from among the adverfaries of Coffee, for no other motive than to fhew from what tales fo learned a man confeffes he fupports a notion, that Coffee (like 'Tea to the Chinefe) acted as a great drier to the *Perfians*, and abated aphrodifiacal warmth. This opinion has been fince received, and propagated from him, as he received and propagated it from its fabulous origin. The facts have been refuted by Sir *Thomas Roe*, and many other travellers.

Sir *Thomas Herbert*, who was in the Eaft in 1626, tells us, that the Perfians themfelves have a very different opinion of Coffee. — " They fay that Coffee comforts the brain, expels melancholy and fleep, purges choler, lightens the fpirits, and begets an excellent concoction; and by cuftom becomes delicious. But all thefe virtues do not conciliate their liking of it fo much as the romantic notion, that it was firft invented and brewed by the Angel *Gabriel*, to reftore *Mahomet's* decayed moifture; which it did fo effectually, that he never drank

drank it but he made nothing to unhorfe forty men, and in his amours to rival the fame of Hercules *."

MANY have been the dogmas concerning Coffee : fome authors alledge that it is *dry*, and therefore good for the grofs and phlegmatic, but hurtful to lean people ; fome contend that it is *cold*, and therefore good for fanguine, bilious, and hot conftitutions ; others, that it is *hot*, and therefore bad for the fanguine and bilious, but good for cold conftitutions. Some affure us, that it acts only as a *fedative*; others, that it acts only as a *ftimulant*. With fuch difputants there is no entering the lifts. Medical fcience difclaims their pretenfions, as creations of the imagi-

* Page 311. Ed. 3. Setting afide the hyperbolical part of this Perfian opinion, here is at leaft a tradition, that this liquor was ufed in Arabia in the time of *Mahomet*, whofe flight from *Mecca* was in the year 622. All the ancient nations who made much ufe of the *Legumina* in their diet, prepared many of them by torrefaction ; and it is moft probable, that the Arabians were acquainted with the art of preparing a liquor from the parched or roafted berries of a tree that was indigenous among them, prior to its ufe in Egypt and Perfia, or in any of the neighbouring countries.

nation ;

nation; and transfers their conteſt for deciſion to a Synod of Turkiſh Prieſts.

I AM aware that there are people who are deciſively of opinion, that Coffee is injurious " in thin habits and bilious temperaments, in melancholic and hypochondriacal diſorders, and to perſons ſubject to hæmorrhages."— *Willis*, *Cheyne*, and others, as well as *Lewis*, who conceived this notion to have been his own, were in ſome degree of this opinion *.

IN habits ſubject to hæmorrhages, particularly thoſe of the pulmonic and uterine kind, the interdiction of Coffee is every where juſtly admitted †.

I WAS acquainted with a perſon at Leyden, when I was a ſtudent there, who ſeldom drank much Coffee, or continued the uſe of it for ſeveral days ſucceſſively, without having an hæmorrhage from the noſe.

* Ab hac ſorbitione abſtinere debent bilioſi, quibus præfervida ſunt viſcera, qui hæmorrhoidibus quibuſcunque eryſipelati ſunt obnoxii, melancholici, et hypochondriaci. *Geoffry*, De Vegetab. Tom. II. ſect. 1. p. 437.

† Yet Dr. *Percival* ſays, it is " powerfully ſedative." Vol. I. p. 127.

BUT

But the other exceptions, however they may have been taken up, and afferted in England, where the confined ufe of Coffee has fcarcely afforded a fair opportunity to fettle fuch a point, will be difputed in countries where it is in general ufe. Let me add alfo, that the refult of my obfervations in thofe countries is evidence againft the exceptions; and it is confirmed by every information I have obtained from medical people refident in Conftantinople, and other parts of the Turkifh Empire.

Let us examine this arbitrary reftriction to the ufe of Coffee, and fee what juftice there is in the principle on which it has been impofed; to which, as to all arbitrary impofitions, we fhall difcover no reafon, I believe, in fubmitting.

In regard to " thin habits," where there is no difeafe, or conftitutional defect, I can fay but little; knowing no theory that militates againft the prudent ufe of Coffee in the alimentary way; nor why it fhould not be as harmlefs to fuch habits, as to thofe who

are

are formed with the greateſt obeſity and rotundity of figure.

TRAVELLERS obſerve, that in Turkey, though the Mahometans and the Greeks live in the ſame towns, they differ widely in their manner of living; and in nothing more than in their drinks. The Turks, whoſe principal drink is Coffee, and one of the articles with which every Turk is obliged to furniſh his wife, are fat, freſh, active, healthy, and prolific. The Greeks, on the contrary, who drink but little Coffee, and much wine, are dry, bilious, paſſionate, and indolent.

IN " bilious temperaments," facts and experience muſt determine. Bilious temperaments are ſurely no where ſo common as in hot climates; and in thoſe very countries Coffee is certainly moſt uſed. There Coffee is found to temper and ſoften the acrimony of the bile, and prepare the ſtomach for purgatives, and ſuitable medicines. It is obſerved in bilious habits, that the ſtomach receives nothing more agreeable than Coffee, unleſs where there is febrile heat; and that the nauſea and inclination

to

to vomit, which often accompany bilious complaints, are taken away by Coffee. In the jaundice, and in obſtructions of the liver, it is ſometimes uſed with great benefit.

To the opinion that Coffee is hurtful in " melancholic and hypochondriacal diſorders," a multitude of opinions may be oppoſed ; and its well known power in removing viſceral obſtructions, and exhilarating the ſpirits ; which qualities have been attributed to Coffee ever ſince the uſe of it was known *.

If it be demanded, what general deſcription of people ſhould abſtain from the uſe of Coffee ?— as it ſeems with ſome people to be neceſſary for the rightly underſtanding its virtues to have ſomething ſaid againſt it,— I muſt anſwer, that I know of none ; yet I wiſh to be underſtood, that I think animadverting on its properties and effects may take

* " Il remedie très efficacement dans les deux ſexes, à toutes les eſpéces d'indiſpoſitions qu'on attribuë aux vapeurs du foye, de la ratte, et de la matrice, et par conſéquent aux maladies hypocondriaques, et généralement à toutes les paſſions hyſteriques," &c. *De Blegny,* p. 177.

place

place, without the writer's being in the predicament of Monf. *de la Clofure* at Perigueux, who ordered it for all his patients becaufe he liked it himfelf; or of Monf. *Barbarec* at Montpellier, who forbad it to his patients becaufe it difagreed with him. Thefe phyficians, like *Mahomet*, incurred the imputation of mixing their inclinations with their prefcriptions.—*Mahomet* prohibited the ufe of wine, becaufe it difordered him, and brought on the epilepfy.

EVERY reafonable perfon muft know, that Coffee cannot be proper for all conftitutions, and at all times. The exceptions may be numerous; but I fhould make a bad figure in the eyes of travellers, who have witneffed abfurdity enough on this fubject, were I, in difcuffing the dietetic regimen of a nation, to attempt to fix invariable rules for individuals.

PEOPLE obnoxious to hæmorrhages, or poffeffing peculiar nervous fenfibility, or feverifh irritability, fhould abftain from all ftimulating liquors; therefore from Coffee.— Thofe who, from their own proper expe-

g   rience,

rience, find it does not agree with them, can hardly ftand in need of this injunction *.

It is well known, that there are fome habits which cannot endure any thing that increafes the fenfibility of the nerves; and others that are affected by particular ftimulants. A cup of ftrong Coffee will caufe fome people to have a tremor of the hand.—*Boyle* fays it acted as an emetic with one perfon; *Galland* was alfo an inftance, where it occafioned the fame operation in a moft violent manner. Others will be heated, or be kept from fleeping by it. Tea, Champagne and Burgundy wines, and many other things, will produce fimilar effects. It was on this account that *Slare*, and fome others, have confounded the excefs of nervous fenfibility with the palfy, which depends on a privation of fenfibility, or motion; —againft

* " Je fcay qu'il fe trouve indifféremment entre les bilieux, les fanguins, les pituiteux, et les melancholiques, des perfonnes à qui il fait du bien, et d'autres à qui il fait du mal; c'eft pourquoy bien qu'il foit vray qu'il y aye peu d'alimens ny de medicamens fi généralement bon que le Caffé." *De Blegny,* p. 105.

which

which nothing appears to be more suitable than Coffee *·

A SUBJECT like Coffee, poſſeſſed of active principles and evident operations, muſt necef-ſarily be capable of miſapplication and abuſe; and there muſt be particular habits which theſe operations diſturb. In ſome it cauſes an inſupportable acidity in the ſtomach.—*Slare* ſays, he uſed Coffee in exceſs, and it affected his nerves †; but Dr. *Fothergill,* who was a

ſenſible

---

* " *Reſolutio nervorum* — interdum tota corpora, in-terdum partes infeſtat. Veteres Authores illud ἀποπληξιαν, hoc παραλυσιν nominaverunt." *Celſ.* Lib. III. cap. 27.

" Privatio eſt ſenſus et motus, in toto corpore, vel parte quadam." *Aret.* Lib. I. cap. 7.

† *Slare,* having inſtanced himſelf as one with whom Coffee did not agree, has miſled many people; and as this circumſtance is ſometimes quoted to juſtify objections againſt Coffee, I beg leave to relate his account of it in his own words:—" Nor do I decry and condemn Coffee, though it proved very prejudicial to my own health, and brought paralytic affections upon me. I confeſs, in my younger days I ignorantly uſed it *in too great exceſs*; as many daily do make uſe of this, and other Indian drinks. Though I have quite abandoned it for above thirty years, and ſoon recovered the good tone of my nerves, which continue ſteady to this day; yet I muſt own, Coffee to

ſome

fenfible man, and had read *Paul's* advice to *Timothy* refpecting wine, and did not ufe Coffee in excefs, though he was of a very delicate habit, and could not ufe Tea, fays, in his letter to *Ellis*, that he drank Coffee " almoft conftantly many years, without receiving any inconveniency from it."

De la Closure fays, that Monf. *Ferrand*, Dean of the Faculty at Limoges, took Coffee every night to make him fleep. The celebrated Monf. *Colbert* drank Coffee to keep him awake, through his great preffure of bufinefs; and by that means fo habituated himfelf to live without reft, that at length he could not fleep when he wanted.

But the hiftory of particular cafes ferves only to prove, that mankind are not all organized alike; and that the fympathy of one, and antipathy of another, are amply provided for in that infinite variety which pervades all na-

fome people is of good ufe, when taken in juft proportion, &c." " It is true that they (Indian drinks) do not agree with all conftitutions; with fome, only one of thefe entertaining liquids, as Green Tea; and with others, all of them difagree."—This candid relation of *Slare's*, requires no comment.

ture,

ture, and with which the earth is bleſſed in the vegetable creation.—Were it not ſo, phyſic would acquire but little aid from the toils of philoſophy, when philoſophy had no other incitement to labour, than barren ſpeculation.

It has long been a cuſtom with many people among us, to add muſtard to their Coffee: muſtard or aromatics may with great propriety be added, in flatulent, languid, and ſcorbutic conſtitutions; and particularly by invalids, and in ſuch caſes where warmth or ſtimulus is required.

The Eaſtern nations add either cloves, cinnamon, cardamoms, cummin-feed, or eſſence of amber, &c. but neither milk or fugar. Milk and fugar without the aromatics, are generally uſed with it in Europe, America, and the Weſt India Iſlands, except when taken immediately after dinner; then the method of the French is often followed, and the milk is omitted.

Coffee is moſt grateful to the ſtomach, as well as to the palate, with the addition of cream, and ſweetened with fugar-candy. The
fugar-

fugar-candy fhould be reduced to a grofs pow-
der, to facilitate its diffolving.

A SMALL cup or two of Coffee, immediately after dinner, promotes digeftion.

HOWEVER, Coffee after dinner, in general,
is to be confidered as a luxury ; and its effects
are then moft pleafant where temperance has
been obferved, and leguminous food and light
wines have chiefly compofed the repaft.

WITH a draught of water previoufly drunk,
according to the Eaftern cuftom, Coffee is
ferviceable to thofe who are of a coftive
habit.

COFFEE is not proper where there has been
long fitting after dinner, when heavy meals of
animal food have been made, and much Por-
tugal wine, has been drunk ; and never fhould
be ufed after dinner, nor at any other time,
by thofe who intend to return to the bottle,
and drink wine immediately upon it.

THUS far the properties and medicinal
effects of Coffee, after torrefaction, have been
confidered ; and as the beverage made from it

contains all the effential virtues of the berry,
which united are moft proper for dietetic purpofes, I have not entered into any difcuffion of
its component parts feparately, nor of the dif-
tilled water, fyrup, oil, and other fimple preparations which have been made from the berry;
for I do not believe, that thefe preparations
poffefs any properties deferving particular
notice; but that we are indebted to the
virtues we derive from Coffee, to the total
derangement of its natural ftate, by the procefs it undergoes in roafting at the fire.—
And therefore the fabulous ftory of the firft
difcovery of its effects, does not merit the
leaft attention.

THE mode of preparing this beverage for
common ufe differs in different countries,
principally as to the additions made to it.—
But though that is generally underftood,
and that tafte, conftitution, the quality of
the Coffee, and the quantity intended to be
drunk, muft be confulted, in regard to the
proportion of Coffee to the water in making
it — yet there is one material point, the importance of which is not well underftood,
and which admits of no deviation.
THE

The prefervation of the virtues of Coffee, particularly when it is of a fine quality, and exempt from ranknefs, as has been faid, depends on carefully confining it after it has been roafted; and not powdering it until the time of ufing it, that the volatile and æthereal principles, generated by the fire, may not efcape. But all this will fignify nothing, and the beft materials will be ufelefs, unlefs the following important admonition is ftrictly attended to; which is, that after the liquor is made, — *it fhould be bright and clear, and entirely exempt from the leaft cloudinefs or foul appearance, from a fufpenfion of any of the particles of the fubftance of the Coffee.*

There is fcarcely any vegetable infufion or decoction, whofe effects differ from its grofs origin more than that of which we are fpeaking. Coffee taken in fubftance caufes oppreffion at the ftomach, heat, naufea, and indigeftion : confequently a continued ufe of a preparation of it, in which any quantity of its fubftance is contained, befides being difgufting to the palate, muft tend to produce the fame indifpofitions. The

refiduum

refiduum of the roafted berry, after its virtues are extracted from it, is little more
than an earthy calx, and muft therefore be
injurious.

THE want of attention to this circumftance, I make no doubt, has been the caufe
of many of the complaints againft Coffee,
and of the averfion which fome people have
to it; and it is from this confideration that
Coffee fhould not be prepared with milk in-
ftead of water, nor fhould the milk be added
to it on the fire, as is fometimes the cafe, for
oeconomical dietetic purpofes, where only a
fmall quantity of Coffee is ufed, as the tena-
city of the milk impedes the precipitation of
the grounds, which is neceffary for the purity
of the liquor, and therefore neither the milk
nor the fugar fhould be added, until after it is
made with water in the ufual way, and the
clarification of it is completed *.—The milk

* It is not to Coffee alone that this reflexion is confined; every article we ufe as a diluter, demands the
fame attention. Malt liquors, particular fmall beer,
which in this refpect is much neglected, ought always to
be carefully fined. The fæculent matter entangled by
the mucilage of the malt, is hurtful to digeftion, and
detrimental to health.

h   fhould

fhould be hot when added to the liquor of
the Coffee, which fhould alfo be hot, or both
fhould be heated together, in this mode of
ufing Coffee as an article of fuftenance.

THE Perfians roaft the membrane which
envelopes the feed, and ufe it together with
the feed itfelf, in their manner of preparing
the infufion, and it is faid to be a confiderable
improvement. The people of fafhion among
the Turks and Perfians make a delicate drink
from the capfules only, which is cooling and
refrefhing; particularly in fummer time.
This was much extolled by the French travellers, who faw no other Coffee ufed at the
houfes of the great. This is called by the
French, *Café à la Sultane.*

THE Turks, Arabians, Perfians, and
Egyptians, drink Coffee all day long, in
fmall cups, fupping it up by a little at a time,
as hot as they can bear it; and what is prepared from three or four ounces among
them, is confidered as a moderate quantity
for one perfon in a day. In the Dutch,
French, and Englifh Colonies, it is the daily
breakfaft and evening repaft.

IF

If a knowledge of the principles of Coffee, founded on examination and various experiments, added to obfervations made on the extenfive and indifcriminate ufe of it, cannot authorize us to attribute to it any particular quality unfriendly to the human frame; — if the unerring teft of experience has confirmed its utility, in many countries, not exclufively productive of thofe inconveniencies, habits, and difeafes, for which its peculiar properties feem moft applicable ;— let thofe properties be duly confidered ; and let us reflect on the ftate of our atmofphere ; the food and modes of life of the inhabitants, — and the chronical infirmities which derive their origin from thefe fources, and it will be evident what falutary effects might be expected from the general dietetic ufe of Coffee in Great Britain.

But this important object cannot be accomplifhed while England frowns on Weft Indian agriculture and commerce.

With legiflative confideration and encouragement, good Coffee would be produced in

2   our

our Weſt Indian Iſlands in ſuch abundance, that, as in France, it might be afforded here at a price to render it a cheap ſubſtitute for thoſe enervating teas and beverages, which the inferior claſſes of people adopt from neceſſity, and which produce the pernicious habit of dram-drinking.

THE increaſed conſumption of the article, for reaſons already urged, would benefit the State ;—and the poor would be ſupplied with an wholeſome ingredient for improving their diet ; which, if we extend our views remote from the Metropolis, will be found ſuch as would admit of much addition and meliora-tion, without any ſuſpicion of the interpoſi-tion of Providence in their favour, or en-dangering the SALUS POPULI on the ſcore of ſuperfluity and luxury.

F I N I S.